The Zebra

Chapter 4
Lesson 62: The Schwa
Lexile® Measure: 560L

Printed in the United States of America

Copyright © September 2012 by Reading Horizons

No part of this publication may be reproduced, stored in a retrieval system, or transmitted in any form or by any means, electronic, mechanical, photocopying, recording, or otherwise, without the prior permission of the copyright owner.

ISBN 978-1-62382-026-8

The zebra is a white-and-black-striped
horse. It lives on the grasslands
of Africa.

No two zebras have stripes that are alike. The stripes help them hide in the brush. They hide from big cats. They hide from other big animals that would eat them.

Zebras do not live alone. They roam along the open grasslands in big herds.

The total number of males and females in a herd are not equal. There is just one adult male and many females. Even though the male looks after the herd, the oldest female decides where the herd will roam. She also decides where the herd will eat. The other zebras always agree with her.

Zebras graze on grass and leaves. They also graze on peelings from trees. They stay by watering holes to drink.

Zebras are silent when they greet one another. They sniff each other's coats. They even scratch one another's backs with their teeth! Most of the time, zebras are polite with each other. But when they get mad, they bite each other's legs.

Zebras like to take dust and mud baths. They roll over in the mud. When the mud dries, they shake it off. The remaining dust protects them from the sun, wind, and bugs.

The zebra is a horse, but it is wild.
People do not ride on zebras. Most
people see them in zoos. Do you
think it would be fun to ride a zebra?

Here is a fun fact: If a zebra sees a wall with black and white stripes painted on it, it will want to stand next to the wall. Does that amaze you?

The End

Comprehension Questions

1. This passage tells about
    a. a wild animal that lives in Africa.
    b. things to do on an African safari.
    c. many kinds of animals that you can see at the zoo.

2. How do zebras greet each other?
    a. With a high five.
    b. They touch noses.
    c. By sniffing each other.

3. Which thing is NOT wild?
    a. a tall building
    b. an untamed horse
    c. a lion in the wilderness

4. What is most likely true about zebras?

    a. They don't like other zebras.

    b. They could not live with penguins.

    c. People think zebras look like elephants.

5. What is a possible reason for a zebra to stand next to a wall painted with black and white stripes?

    a. It wants to show off.

    b. To pose for a picture

    c. It is used to standing next to other zebras.

Skill Words

adult	another*	open	total
agree	another's*	other*	zebra
alike	decides	other's*	zebras
alone	equal	protects	
amaze	even*	silent	

Most Common Words

a	get	not	them
after	have	number	there
also	help	of	they
and	her	oldest	think
another*	here	on	to
another's*	if	one	two
are	in	other*	want
backs	is	other's*	watering
be	it	over	when
big	just	people	where
but	like	see	will
by	live	sees	with
do	lives	she	would
does	looks	take	you
each	many	that	
even*	most	the	
from	no	their	

Challenge Words

Africa	though
always	zoos
animals	
herd	
herds	
horse	

*both Skill Word and Most Common Word